FRIENDS AROUND THE WORLD

ACTIVITY BOOK

Visit Tyndale's website for kids at www.tyndale.com/kids.

Visit the Compassion Explorer website at https://explorer.compassion.com.

See all Tyndale and Compassion products at www.everyoneneedscompassion.com.

TYNDALE is a registered trademark of Tyndale House Publishers, Inc. The Tyndale Kids logo is a trademark of Tyndale House Publishers, Inc.

Compassion and Compassion International® are registered trademarks of Compassion International,® Inc.

Friends Around the World Activity Book

Copyright © 2019 by Compassion International.® All rights reserved.

Some of the content in this book originally appeared in the *Compassion Explorer* magazine,® copyright © Compassion International.®

Photos of children in the developing world by Chuck Bigger, copyright © Compassion International.®

Crafts and recipes photos by Josh Lewis, Callie Wilburn, and Sally Dunn, copyright © Compassion International.®

Content written by Gwen Hersha, Leanna Summers, and Willow Welter

Designed by Jennifer L. Phelps

Illustrations by Jacob Souva/Astound US Inc. Copyright © Tyndale House Publishers, Inc. All rights reserved.

All Scripture quotations, unless otherwise indicated, are taken from the Holy Bible, *New International Version,*® *NIV.*® Copyright © 1973, 1978, 1984, 2011 by Biblica, Inc.® Used by permission. All rights reserved worldwide.

Scripture quotations marked NLT are taken from the *Holy Bible*, New Living Translation, copyright © 1996, 2004, 2015 by Tyndale House Foundation. Used by permission of Tyndale House Publishers, Inc., Carol Stream, Illinois 60188. All rights reserved.

Scripture quotations marked ICB are taken from the International Children's Bible.®
Copyright © 1986, 1988, 1999 by Thomas Nelson, Inc. Used by permission. All rights reserved.

For manufacturing information regarding this product, please call 1-800-323-9400.

For information about special discounts for bulk purchases, please contact Tyndale House Publishers at csresponse@tyndale.com, or call 1-800-323-9400.

ISBN 978-1-4964-2601-7

Printed in China

25	24	23	22	21	20	19
7	6	5	4	3	2	1

CONTENTS

✕

Give, and you
will receive. You will
be given much. It will
be poured into your
hands—more than you
can hold. You will be
given so much that it
will spill into your lap.
The way you give to
others is the way God
will give to you.

LUKE 6:38, ICB

✕

NOTE TO PARENTS AND TEACHERS

The fun, educational activities, crafts, and recipes in this book are designed to bring your family or class together in meaningful ways as the children in your life learn more about impoverished children in the developing world.

Becoming aware of others and their needs is the first step toward loving them and bringing them hope and help.

Poverty is not just about lacking financial resources; it has implications for every area of life. A wheel can serve as a representation of the problem of poverty around the world. The hub represents absolute poverty. The spokes represent the different needs of those in poverty: social, health, spiritual, environmental, educational, and economic. The rim represents enough. When we live from a place of enough, we have the opportunity to engage with people in different contexts and then share what we have.

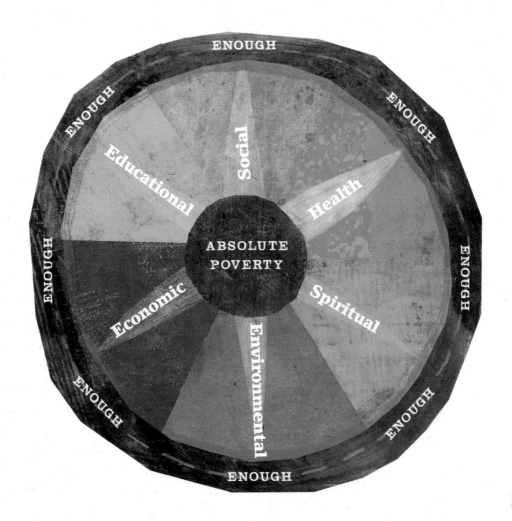

The world is complex and diverse, but when we look at people through the lens of God's great love, it doesn't take long to recognize that we are very much alike. This activity book is designed to help you lead your family or class in this discovery.

The book is arranged in six sections, each of which will help the children in your life see how children in the developing world experience some of the same things they experience. Each section is packed with activities, puzzles, and crafts to help children develop understanding and compassion for others and their needs. An introduction to each section helps you focus on the following categories through the perspective of Scripture and truth.

1. Family and Friends (Social)   **4.** School (Educational)
2. Home (Environmental)   **5.** Church (Spiritual)
3. Food and Water (Health)   **6.** Clothing and Toys (Economic)

Here are some ways you can use this book to help your children learn about and develop compassionate hearts toward the poor:

➡ Choose one of the parts of the book and lead a group of children through the activities. Then help them take action to reach out to families living in poverty. Finally, celebrate your project and what you learned with others.

➡ Schedule a time to do an activity from the book one day each week. Complete a project together, and then decide on ways you can reach out to people in the world who need help.

➡ Plan a cultural day for each month. Select a craft, a game, and a recipe to represent life in a particular country or region. Enjoy being creative, playing together, and eating something new. End the day with a prayer for the people living there. Brainstorm ways you can help others, whether as a family or as a class.

A grand adventure awaits as you explore God's heart of compassion and as you develop a heart of compassion yourself. Have fun on this journey of discovery, and may God richly bless your time with your children as you learn and grow together.

Family and Friends

RELATIONSHIPS
AROUND THE WORLD

✕

Speak up for those who cannot speak for themselves; ensure justice for those being crushed. Yes, speak up for the poor and helpless, and see that they get justice.

PROVERBS 31:8-9, NLT

Family and Friends

✱ PART 1

RELATIONSHIPS AROUND THE WORLD

God loves us, and He created us in His own image. This means we can love, communicate with, and care for others—just like He does!

God deeply loves people all over the world. The Bible says, "For God so loved *the world* that he gave his one and only Son, that whoever believes in him shall not perish but have eternal life" (John 3:16, emphasis added).

When we look at one another, we may see differences. We see skin colors different from ours, languages we don't know how to speak, and foods we are afraid to eat. But God sees all the ways we are the same. The more we learn about those who are different from us, the more we will see our similarities and understand His great love for the whole world.

While you are enjoying the games and projects in this section, think about the similarities you have with children from other countries. For example, all over the world, families have to do laundry. In the activity "Hanging Together," the clothespins you turn into fun characters can remind you of the way God has created each person in His image. As you make the "Give a Hoot!" owls, remember that just like children in poverty, you can create something special with scraps you find around your house.

1

✂ CRAFTS AND ACTIVITIES

Playing games together is a great way to connect with your family and friends. Did you know that kids whose families can't afford to buy checkerboards often get creative and make their own? Learn how you can too!

✚ Supplies

- 1 large empty cereal box
- 1-inch hole punch (optional)
- craft paint (two colors)
- 1 piece of sturdy cardboard (12 inches by 12 inches)
- 1 ruler
- nontoxic water-based paints or markers

☰ Directions

1. Using the empty box, cut out 24 circles (one inch across). You can also punch out 24 circles using a hole punch.
2. Paint 12 of the circles one color and 12 of the circles another color.
3. Using your ruler, draw lines on the cardboard, dividing it into 64 squares. Each square should be 1 ½ inches across.
4. Use paint or markers to color in the checkerboard so that no two squares side by side are the same color. (You can also leave half of the squares the color of the cardboard.)

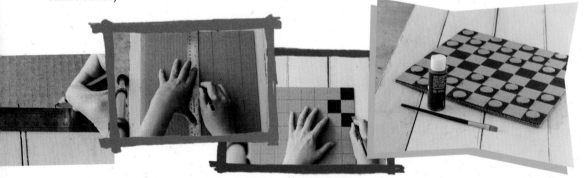

GIVE A HOOT!

These fun creatures can be made with recycled materials. Consider giving one of them to a family member or friend to show kindness to someone you know.

✚ Supplies

- 1 cardboard tube from a toilet paper roll
- 1 sheet of paper (any color)
- markers
- safety scissors
- glue
- googly eyes (optional)

≡ Directions

1. Fold the top of the cardboard tube toward the middle so it resembles an owl's head.
2. For wings, draw two almond shapes on the paper. The wings should be slightly smaller in length than the tube. If you're using white paper, color the shapes with markers. Then cut out the wings.
3. For the beak, draw a triangle on a piece of orange paper, or draw a triangle on white paper and color it in with orange marker. Cut it out.
4. Glue the beak to the front of the tube, and glue wings to the sides of the tube. Draw big eyes with a marker, or glue on some googly eyes.

MORE OPTIONS:
For a more colorful owl, paint the cardboard tube and let it dry before adding wings, a beak, and eyes. You could also cut the tube in half to make two baby owls.

HANGING TOGETHER

Many families living in poverty can't afford dryers, so they hang their laundry on clotheslines. This summer, consider drying your clothes on a line too. In this activity, you can decorate clothespins to look like your family members and then use them to hang up your clothes.

Supplies

- wooden clothespins
- googly eyes
- feathers in multiple colors (yellow, brown, black, and red)
- felt in multiple colors
- wood glue
- permanent marker

Directions

1. Using googly eyes and markers, make a face on the closed end of the clothespin.
2. On top of the closed end of the clothespin, glue on feathers for hair.
3. Use different colors of felt or markers to make an outfit on the open end of the clothespin.
4. Repeat the steps to decorate more clothespins like yourself and other family members. Then use your clothespin people to hang your wet laundry on a clothesline!

LET FRIENDSHIP BLOOM

Giving flowers to someone is a sign of kindness and friendship. Using these instructions, you can create one flower or a whole bouquet. And these flowers don't cost much—you can even reuse tissue paper from gifts you've received!

Supplies

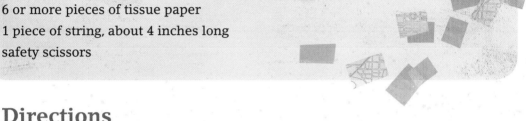

- 6 or more pieces of tissue paper
- 1 piece of string, about 4 inches long
- safety scissors

Directions

1. Stack at least 6 sheets of colorful tissue paper on top of one another. Then fold the stack of paper lengthwise to make a 1-inch pleat.
2. Use your first fold as a guide to make accordion pleats. Flip over the stack of tissue paper and make a fold the same size as your first one. Continue this step until you've reached the end of the paper and have a rectangular strip that resembles an accordion.
3. Tie the string around the middle of the tissue strip. Don't worry about loose ends; they'll be hidden in the flower.
4. Use scissors to cut both edges of the tissue strip. Rounded edges will make round petals, and pointed edges will make pointy petals.
5. To open the flower, gently pull layers of tissue paper toward the center, one at a time.

MORE OPTIONS:
To make a hanging flower, use a ribbon in place of the string. To add a stem, use a pipe cleaner in place of the string.

ONE-OF-A-KIND PHOTO FRAME

Photos are a great way to remember the people we love. This activity could also be a way to show a friend how much you care for him or her!

Supplies

- photo of your family or friend
- 1 piece of construction paper (any color)
- safety scissors
- glue stick
- markers

Directions

1. Find a photo of your family or a friend that you want to frame.
2. Cut out a construction border that is at least an inch larger than the picture.
3. Glue the picture in the center of the construction paper frame. Let dry.
4. Decorate the frame with your favorite Bible verse.
5. Hang the picture on your refrigerator or give it to a friend.

PIECES OF THE WHOLE

A tangram is a traditional Chinese puzzle that is made of shapes. These shapes can be arranged to look like animals, boats, or other figures. As you make this magnetic tangram set, think about how every shape sticks together to create a complete picture—just like each person makes up a special family.

+ Supplies

- tangram pattern (p. 104 in the back of the book)
- tangram idea guide
- printer
- 1 sheet of magnetic paper (found at office-supply or craft stores)
- safety scissors
- foam brush
- clear acrylic sealer, such as Mod Podge
- 1 tin with a lid, such as an empty Altoids container

═ Directions

1. Scan the tangram pattern and idea guide at the back of the book and print them out onto the magnetic paper. Cut out the square tangram pattern and the idea guide.
2. With the foam brush, coat the front of the pattern, idea guide, and tin cover with acrylic sealer.
3. When the sealer has dried, carefully cut out the shapes in the tangram pattern.
4. Stick the idea guide magnet to the bottom of the tin. Stick the magnetic shapes to the tin's lid.
5. Now your tangram is ready to play with. Arrange the shapes so they look like the pictures in the idea guide, or make your own pictures!

* Find the tangram template on p. 104 in the back of the book.

⊞ PUZZLES

⟩ TRUE TREASURES

The word treasure means "a person or thing considered very valuable." Some treasures, like toys and jewelry, are earthly things that don't last forever. Others, like family and friends, are treasures of the heart. In the blanks next to the coins below, name some of the treasures in your life. Then draw a line from each treasure to the chest where it would be kept—in an earthly chest or in your heart. Which treasures are most important to you? Why?

● _____   ● _____

● _____   ● _____

● _____   ● _____

● _____   ● _____

● _____   ● _____

EARTHLY CHEST

YOUR HEART

Here's what coins look like in some countries where Compassion works with children.

| BANGLADESHI TAKA | DOMINICAN PESO | KENYAN SHILLING | RWANDAN FRANC |

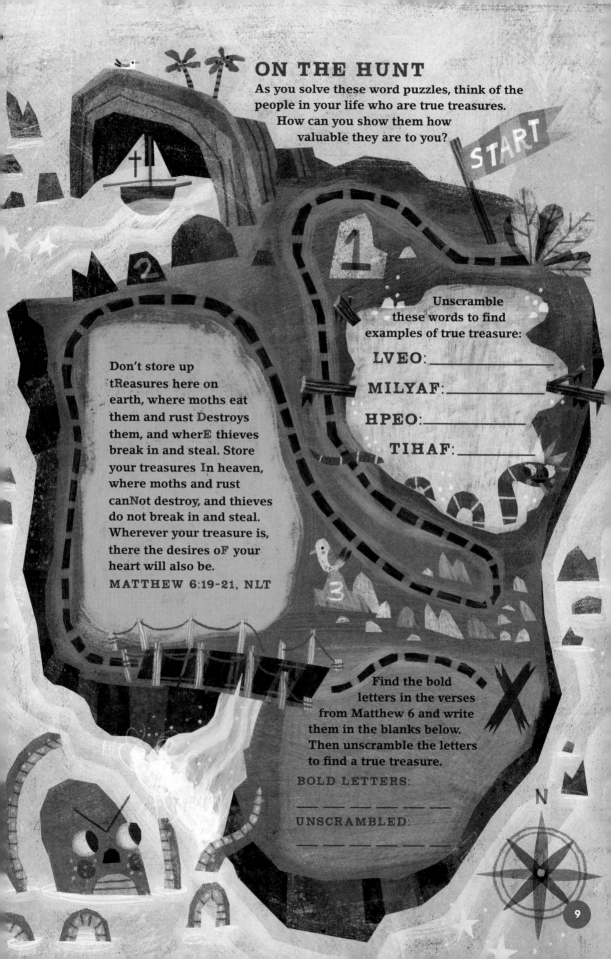

ON THE HUNT

As you solve these word puzzles, think of the people in your life who are true treasures. How can you show them how valuable they are to you?

START

Unscramble these words to find examples of true treasure:

LVEO: _____

MILYAF: _____

HPEO: _____

TIHAF: _____

Don't store up tReasures here on earth, where moths eat them and rust Destroys them, and wherE thieves break in and steal. Store your treasures In heaven, where moths and rust canNot destroy, and thieves do not break in and steal. Wherever your treasure is, there the desires oF your heart will also be.

MATTHEW 6:19-21, NLT

Find the bold letters in the verses from Matthew 6 and write them in the blanks below. Then unscramble the letters to find a true treasure.

BOLD LETTERS:

___ ___ ___ ___ ___ ___

UNSCRAMBLED:

___ ___ ___ ___ ___ ___

ACTION STEPS

1. READ MICAH 6:8 out loud together.

> He has shown you, O mortal, what is good.
> And what does the Lord require of you?
> To act justly and to love mercy
> and to walk humbly with your God.
>
> **MICAH 6:8**

What do you think it means to act justly? What does it mean to love mercy? As a family or a class, figure out a way you can show justice and mercy to someone this week:

_____

_____

_____

_____

_____

_____

_____

_____

2. WRITE A NOTE TO A FRIEND to show them that you treasure them. You can use the ideas below to get you started.

DEAR _____

I want you to know that I treasure you—and so does God! I value you because you are _____. I like the way you _____, and I think it's cool that you _____!

Someone else in my life I really treasure is _____ because _____. Who do you treasure?

I think that people are so much more important than things, because _____. But I still like to play with my _____. What is your favorite thing to play with?

YOUR FRIEND,

_____

PART 2

Home

HOUSES AROUND THE WORLD

Lord, through all the generations you have been our home!

Before the mountains were born, before you gave birth to the earth and the world, from beginning to end, you are God.

PSALM 90:1-2, NLT

Home

HOUSES AROUND THE WORLD

What do you think is needed for a good home? You might be thinking about a floor, walls, a roof, and windows. Maybe your list includes things like a kitchen, a bathroom, a playroom, a backyard, and bedrooms. Houses give shelter from the sun, the rain, the cold, the wind, and the snow.

The poorest children in the world don't have a safe place to call home. They may have a place to sleep, but their homes may not have space to play, study, or eat. Children in the developing world often live in shelters that aren't very sturdy and are made from pieces of cardboard, scraps of metal, or cheap concrete blocks. When there are heavy rains or strong winds, their homes fall apart. Most of these shelters have only one room, and they don't have electricity or a heater or running water.

The activities in this section will help you think about how children in the developing world live and remind you to pray for them. For example, you can use recycled materials to make a shoebox shelter that looks like one that kids in the developing world might live in. When you make your own candles, you can think about and pray for kids who don't have electricity and have to use candles or kerosene lamps to study.

Whether we have a one-room shelter or a house with our own room, there's one thing we know for sure: God is our shelter. He is always with us. He keeps us safe from harm and gives us good things. And someday we will live in the home that God has prepared for us in heaven!

✂ CRAFTS AND ACTIVITIES

HOMEMADE SOAP

It's important to wash your hands with soap because soap gets rid of germs that make people sick. You probably buy soap from the store, but many children in developing countries have learned to make their own. You can follow these instructions to make your own soap too! (These supplies can be found at most craft stores.)

➕ Supplies

- glycerin soap bars (clear or white)
- soap dye in your favorite colors (optional)
- candy molds or soap molds
- microwave-safe measuring cup
- spoon
- knife (Be sure to ask an adult for help!)

═ Directions

1. Cut a glycerin soap bar into two or three squares and place them in the measuring cup.
2. Microwave the soap pieces for about 20 seconds or until melted.
3. If you want colored soap, add a few drops of dye to the melted soap and stir with a spoon. If you want a darker color, add more dye. If the liquid starts to harden, microwave it until it's melted again.
4. Slowly pour the melted soap into a mold. Set it aside to let it harden for about an hour.
5. Rinse out the measuring cup and repeat the steps for other colors and molds.
6. After the soap is cooled, pop it out of the mold. If you have trouble getting it out, try putting it in the freezer for ten minutes and then try again.

TIPS:
For a swirled look, wait to add the dye until after you pour the white soap into a mold. Then add a few drops of dye to the soap in the mold and swirl it around with a toothpick.

For layers of different colors, pour the first color into the mold and let it cool for about five minutes. Then slowly add the second color over it.

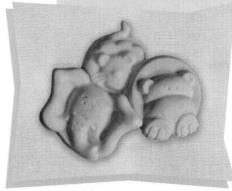

Most of us have electricity in our homes to power our lights, ovens, and refrigerators. Many kids in developing countries don't have electricity, so they use candles or kerosene lamps after it gets dark. Try making your own candles (but make sure you ask an adult for help).

+ Supplies

- wick (these can be found at craft stores) or a piece of cotton string
- scissors
- baby bottle or other plastic bottle with a wide opening
- wax (you can use melted wax from old candles or buy wax at a craft store)
- 4 cups water

Directions

1. Cut the wick so that it's at least 4 inches longer than the bottle.
2. Fill the plastic bottle almost all the way to the top with pieces of wax.
3. Bring water to a boil in a large pot and then place the bottle of wax in the water.
4. When the wax has melted, remove the bottle and place it on your work surface.
5. Lower all but about 4 inches of the wick into the wax. Remove the wick slowly and count to five (the wax will stick to the wick).
6. Continue holding the wick and dipping in the wax until you're happy with how your candle looks.
7. Hang the candle by its wick (you can tie it to a clothesline or a hanger) and let it dry for at least three hours.
8. Trim the wick to about a half-inch long.

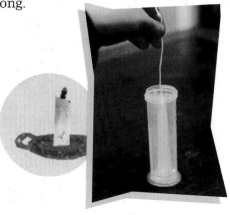

SHOEBOX SHELTER

Shelter is a basic need because it helps protect people from bad weather and danger. Recycle a box and an egg carton to make a mini version of what a home in a developing country might look like. (Be sure to ask an adult for help with this activity.)

✚ Supplies

- shoe box or other small box
- utility knife such as X-Acto (optional)
- markers or crayons
- scissors
- egg carton (empty)
- glue
- acrylic craft paint
- paintbrush

≡ Directions

1. Have an adult use the utility knife to cut out small squares in the shoebox. These will be windows for your mini home. Or you can draw on windows using markers or crayons.
2. On the inside of your box, draw items that might be found on the walls of a home, such as clothes, pictures, or dishes.
3. Now make the furniture for the house using the egg carton. Cut pieces of the top and bottom into seats, a table, and a bed.
4. Paint your furniture in bright colors, let it dry, and then fill your home!

UNFORGETTABLE WATERING CAN

An elephant never forgets—and you'll never forget to water your plants once you make this watering can! When we need something for our home, most of us go to the store to buy it. But people in the developing world don't always have the resources to buy something new, so they learn to get creative. This watering can is similar to something a person in the developing world would create since it's made from reused items that might otherwise end up in the trash. (Be sure to ask an adult for help with this activity.)

+ Supplies

- 2 empty milk jugs (1 gallon each)
- utility knife such as X-Acto or scissors
- craft foam
- hot glue gun
- 2 googly eyes

≡ Directions

1. For the trunk, cut off the handle of one jug, leaving an edge around each end of the handle. Around one of those edges, cut a ring of slits about a ¼ inch deep and ¼ inch apart. (You won't use the rest of this jug.)
2. Remove the cap from the other jug and cut a dime-size hole in the center. Replace the cap and set the jug handle-side up.
3. To attach the trunk, carefully put a line of glue around the outside of the cap. Then wrap the slit end of the trunk around the cap. Make sure the trunk is pointing up and that the cap doesn't get glued to the jug.
4. For the ears, cut out two large circles of craft foam. For the eyes, cut out two circles that are a little bigger than the googly eyes. Glue the large circles to the sides of the jug.
5. Glue the small circles on each side of the handle. Then glue the googly eyes to the small circles.
6. After the glue has dried, you can fill the jug with water by removing the cap. Now you're ready to water plants!

Rugs can help keep floors cleaner and warmer, especially for homes with dirt floors. This rug can be made from old bedsheets, strips of old towels, or other fabrics.

✛ Supplies

- ruler
- marker
- piece of sturdy cardboard (at least 16 inches wide)
- scissors
- bedsheet or other recycled fabric

☰ Directions

1. Use a ruler and a marker to mark half-inch segments across the long side of the cardboard. Slit the cardboard at the marks, cutting about 3 inches down. This creates notches that will grip the fabric.

2. Cut the bedsheet into six strips, about 2 inches wide and at least 4 feet long. Set aside. Then cut the rest of the sheet into strips 2 inches wide and at least 2 feet long.

3. Stack three of the shorter strips on top of one another to make one thick strip. Slide the thick strip into one cardboard notch, leaving 3 inches hanging off one side. Repeat with three shorter strips in each slot. These are your base strips.

4. Stack two of the longer strips on top of one another to make one thick weaving strip. Slide into the first cardboard notch, leaving 3 inches hanging off one side.

5. Slide the weaving strip under the first set of three base strips, then over the second set, and so on. When you get to the end of the first row, tighten the weave by tugging on the strips. Then weave the other way. If you run out of weaving strip, weave the end into the other strips. Resume weaving with a new set of two longer strips.

6. Weave at least 15 rows. Then tie the end of the weaving strip to a base strip. Tie each loose strip to another, and cut loose strips to make fringe. Slide off the cardboard and repeat on the top side.

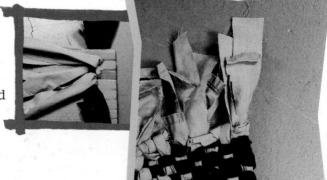

🧩 PUZZLES

➡ SAME DIFFERENCE

Your average day might be very different from the average day of a kid in another country. But no matter how different your surroundings are, there are lots of things you have in common too! As you participate in these activities, talk about ways you are similar to and different from kids in other countries.

The words in this word search are things that kids everywhere should have but kids living in poverty often are missing. Find these words:

CLEAN WATER   **SCHOOLS**   **STURDY HOUSES**
FOOD   **CLOTHES**
MEDICINE   **PLAYGROUNDS**

```
S M O F H M G Q I X S D I C
P D O U Z W Z S Z U Q W R L
P O N S E G U R O M L Z E O
D D Q U C S J P T F P W T T
S E S U O H Y D R U T S A H
Z G J K G R O C H L V N W E
Q R R Q T F G O O S G P N S
W R C I F K A Y L K O R A I
M E D I C I N E A S H S E C
U Z R J W M P V C L H W L E
Y M J N O U C Q F W P B C O
```

HIDING IN TANZANIA

Tanzania is a country in East Africa. If you live in the United States, that's more than 7,000 miles away! But even though these countries are far apart, they have a lot in common. Both places have animals, cars, plants, houses, food, and water—although in Tanzania, those things look a little different from how they look in the United States.

Find the following objects you'd see in Tanzania that you probably wouldn't see where you live:

 SAUSAGE TREE: The poisonous fruit looks like a sausage!

 MOSQUITO NET: This net provides protection against malaria.

 GOAT AND COW: The Maasai people of Tanzania raise livestock to trade or to eat.

 CHAPATI: Tanzanian kids love this flatbread.

 WATER WELL: Most people pump water by hand instead of turning on a faucet.

 DALA DALA: This minibus is used as a taxi in cities.

 MUD HOME: Maasai houses are built of mud, sticks, and grass.

TRICKY TRAIL

Play this game to see what a normal day is like for a kid growing up in Uganda (a country in East Africa). How is it different from your life? How is it similar?

SUPPLIES

1 six-sided die

4 stand-up players *(find these on p. 105 at the back of the book)*

WATER HOLE 3 MI.

You have to walk a long way to get water. **STAY HERE** until next turn.

START

A mosquito bites you, putting you at risk for malaria. **LOSE YOUR NEXT TURN.**

FINISH

Say "good night" in Luganda: "Sula bulungi."

You thanked God before dinner. **GO AHEAD 1.**

TEA

You had enough flour to make porridge for the family. **GO AHEAD 1.**

Read Proverbs 31:8-9 out loud. **THEN GO AHEAD 1.**

MARKET. All players **STOP** to buy cassava flour for dinner.

GAME RULES

1. Place the stand-up player tokens on the START space. The player who gets back home first wins!
2. When it's your turn, roll the die and move your game token that number of spaces. Follow the directions for the space you land on. No matter what you roll, stop on all spaces that say "All players STOP." Your turn ends when you get to a STOP space.
3. If the space tells you to move ahead or back, don't follow the directions for the new space. Your turn ends when you reach the new space.

WATER HOLE: All players STOP HERE to fill a jug with water.

You see a snake and run away. GO AHEAD 1.

You get a stomachache from drinking dirty water. GO BACK 1.

SCHOOL: All players STOP for class.

You learn how to do a new math problem. GO AHEAD 1.

Your sponsor writes you a letter! GO AHEAD 1.

You memorize a Bible verse. GO AHEAD 2.

You stand up for a classmate who is getting bullied. GO AHEAD 1.

COMPASSION CENTER: All players STOP for food, water, playtime, tutoring, and Bible lessons.

OPEN HOUSE

Look inside these homes, which are similar to ones many kids in developing countries live in. Families in poverty often don't have enough money or space for things like furniture, appliances, electricity, and running water. How are these homes different from or similar to your home?

FIND THESE HIDDEN ITEMS!

 People without ovens often cook in fire pits.

 This bucket is a filter that makes dirty water safe to drink.

 Some kids without electricity at home do homework by candlelight.

 Not all families can afford safe, comfortable shoes.

 Some kids need glasses to see their surroundings and do well in school.

🦶 ACTION STEPS

→ **1. MANY CHILDREN IN POVERTY** sleep on the floor because their
family can't afford beds or because their home doesn't have enough space for beds.
It's common for large families of six or more people to share a home that is eight
feet by eight feet. Get a yardstick or tape measure and mark out a space that is
eight feet by eight feet. Now imagine if your whole family lived in that space!
One night this week, spend a night on the floor. In the morning, talk about how
you slept. Write about your experience here:

_____

_____

_____

_____

→ **2. MALARIA** is a serious illness spread by
mosquitoes. About three thousand children die
every day as a result of this disease. While
malaria is not found in the United States
anymore, many children in other parts of the world
get the disease because they don't have money to buy mosquito nets. Pray for
children who don't have nets, and ask God to show you other ways you can help
with the problem. Talk about your ideas with your parents or another adult.
Write your ideas here:

_____

_____

_____

_____

_____

_____

PART 3

Food and Water

MEALS AROUND THE WORLD

✕

✕

All creatures look to you
to give them their food
at the proper time.
When you give it to them,
they gather it up;
when you open your hand,
they are satisfied
with good things.

PSALM 104:27-28

✕

✳ PART 3

Food and Water

MEALS AROUND THE WORLD

A lot of people talk about making healthy choices when it comes to what we eat and drink. Maybe your family has made choices to drink less soda or to eat more vegetables or to make sure you get a balanced diet. Parents all over the world want their children to have the nutrition they need to grow up healthy and strong. But many parents in the developing world often don't have enough to eat or enough money for healthful foods.

As you do the activities in this section, you can think about and pray for parents and children who don't have enough to eat and drink. For example, get your family or friends together and play Guardians of Grainsberry, where you'll gather the supplies you'll need to have a meal, clothes, and shelter. When the game is over, talk about what it would be like to live in a family that has very little.

No matter what we need, we can trust that God knows about it, and He loves and cares for us. If we already have what we need to be healthy, we can make a plan to help others.

29

✂ CRAFTS AND ACTIVITIES

MAKE YOUR OWN DIRTLESS GARDEN

In some places, like parts of Peru, the soil is not good for growing crops, so people have learned how to grow food using hydroponics (growing plants in nutrients instead of soil). Try this experiment to see how it works! (Be sure to ask an adult for help with this activity.)

✚ Supplies

- 1 small Swedish ivy plant
- 1 clear, empty plastic water bottle
    (at least 20 ounces)
- wicking material for hydroponics or 1 used
    cotton T-shirt cut into strips
    (about 1" wide and 12" long)
- 1 small bottle of hydroponic nutrients

- sharp scissors or utility knife
- paper towels
- baking soda
- lemon juice
- pH testing kit or litmus paper
- sunny window

═ Directions

1. Clip off several stems from the vine of your plant. Place the clippings in a glass of water for two to three weeks until roots appear from the clippings.
2. Cut off the top of the bottle, about one-fourth of the way down. Fill up the bottom part of the bottle with water.
3. Remove the lid from the top part of the bottle and turn it over so the opening faces down. Wrap the roots of your plant, along with the end of your wicking material or T-shirt material, in several moistened paper towels, and insert through the lid opening. Place this inverted half inside the rest of the bottle. The wick should dangle through the bottle neck into the bottom half of the bottle.
4. Pour ½ to 1 teaspoon of the nutrients into the water.
5. Check the pH level of the water. The pH should be between 5 and 7. If the pH is over 7, add juice from half a lemon per gallon of water. If the pH is 5 or lower, add 1 teaspoon baking soda.
6. Place your hydroponic plant in a sunny window and watch it grow!

+ Supplies

- 1 large clear glass or plastic bowl
- clear plastic wrap
- salt
- food dye (any color)
- tap water
- 1 pebble
- spices that add an unpleasant taste, such as garlic or chili powder (optional)

≡ Directions

1. Assemble your supplies on a table in a sunny spot.
2. In the bowl, mix water, salt, food dye, and spices until the water looks dirty.
3. Place the drinking glass in the center of the bowl.
4. Cover the bowl with the plastic wrap so that it's a little loose. Place the pebble on top of the plastic so it's exactly above the drinking glass.
5. Leave the bowl in the sunshine for two or three hours and check on it regularly to note what is happening. The heat from the sun is trapped by the plastic wrap and is absorbed by the salty water. The heat causes the temperature in the bowl to increase and causes the water to evaporate. The water vapor reaches the plastic sheet, where it forms water. That water runs down the plastic sheet to the pebble and drips into the cup. This water is clean and good to drink!

DID YOU KNOW?
Dirty water makes kids sick. Around the world, more than 1,400 kids younger than five years old die every day from diarrhea caused by drinking dirty water.

BUILD YOUR OWN MUDSLIDE

Have you ever played in the mud? Or made mud pies out of dirt and water? It rains a lot in Asia, which can create very muddy conditions. Mud can be dangerous when a lot of it slides down hills and into homes. Mudslides can damage or even destroy homes that are made out of cardboard, straw, and scraps of wood.

Try this experiment outside to learn more about how mudslides work.

Supplies

- 2 cookie sheets
- small boards (optional)
- potting soil (enough to cover each cookie sheet 1 inch deep)
- several small rocks
- several clumps of grass with roots attached
- a pitcher of water

Directions

1. Lay the cookie sheets on the ground next to each other. Ask a friend to help you prop up one end of each sheet about 2 inches, or find some small boards to prop them up.
2. Cover each sheet with 1 inch of soil.
3. Place the rocks and grass in the soil of one sheet.
4. Hold the pitcher about 5 inches from the top of the first sheet and slowly pour the water so it runs downhill on the soil. Watch what happens. Repeat for the other sheet.

Which sheet had a bigger mudslide? Do you think trees and plants can help prevent mud from sliding too much? Pray for families whose homes are in the path of mudslides.

RAINFOREST IN A BOTTLE

Some children in South America live in cities, and others live high in the mountains or deep in the jungle. Did you know that rainforests are an important part of God's creation? Plants and trees in rainforests recycle and clean water. They even make the air we breathe cleaner! Rainforests also soak up water from heavy rains. The water is slowly released into the atmosphere, and this helps prevent flooding and droughts.

Try this experiment to find out how plants, air, water, and soil work together to create a healthy environment. Then think of all the ways the rainforest helps keep the Earth a great place to live! (Be sure to ask an adult for help with this activity.)

+ Supplies

- clear plastic 2-liter soda bottle and cap (empty)
- a handful of small pebbles
- 1 cup of potting soil (enough to cover about 2 inches of the bottle)
- grass seeds and/or herb seeds
- ¼ cup of water
- a warm, sunny place

= Directions

1. Place a small layer of stones in the bottom of the bottle.
2. Add a layer of potting soil (2 to 3 inches deep).
3. Add the seeds.
4. Add the water.
5. Put the cap on the bottle and place it in a warm, sunny place.
6. Watch the bottle for several days.
7. When the plants begin to grow, you will see drops of water in the bottle. These drop will "rain" down and keep watering your plant seeds!

Every time you look at your mini rainforest, thank God for the way He has made the parts of our world to work together.

A PLACE FOR GIVING THANKS

This Thai-themed place mat will keep your table clean while reminding you to be thankful for food and the other blessings God has given you. Decorate it with the bright colors worn by Thailand's Karen tribe.

+ Supplies

- colorful paper (red, green, and yellow)
- scissors
- markers or crayons
- clear adhesive paper (found in craft stores or home-improvement stores)

≡ Directions

1. Cut the paper into different shapes. You might want to try elephants or parasols to go with the Thai theme. Decorate the shapes with markers or crayons, writing "Give thanks" on at least one shape.
2. Decide what size rectangle you'd like for your place mat, then cut a sheet of adhesive paper into that shape. Cut a second sheet of adhesive paper to the same size.
3. Peel the backing off the first piece of adhesive paper. Press the shapes you cut out to the sticky side of the adhesive paper.
4. Peel down about 2 inches of the backing of the second piece of adhesive paper. Line it up with the first sheet, sticky sides touching. Peel off the rest of the backing as you press the two sheets together.
5. Trim the edges if needed, and then place on the table for your next meal!

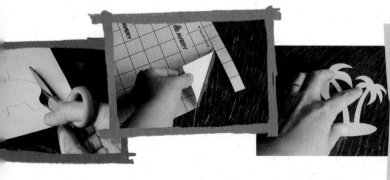

BLESSINGS-MOBILE

Some of the daily gifts God gives us, such as food and water, are easy to overlook. This colorful mobile is a great way to remember the many blessings God pours down on us every day.

Supplies

- 5 or more magazine pictures
- safety scissors
- 1 thick paper plate
- 6 pieces of cardboard from empty food boxes
- clear-drying glue
- hole punch
- 1 long piece of ribbon or yarn (12 inches long)
- 5 pieces of yarn (6–9 inches long)

Directions

1. Choose five pictures from the magazine pages that show how God gives you what you need. Cut them out.
2. Cut the paper plate in half to make an umbrella shape.
3. Cut a handle shape with one piece of cardboard and glue it to the back of your umbrella.
4. Punch five holes around the rim of the umbrella. Punch one hole in the top center so you can lace the long piece of yarn through it to hang from the ceiling or doorpost.
5. Glue each picture to a piece of cardboard. Let dry.
6. Cut around each mounted picture.
7. Punch a hole in the top of each picture and tie a piece of ribbon to the picture hole, then into the holes in your umbrella.
8. Be sure to hang your mobile away from lights or other heat sources.

🧩 PUZZLES

GUARDIANS OF GRAINSBERRY

Raising animals and plants for food or to sell can help people in poverty survive. In this two- or three-player game, pretend your family lives in the make-believe village of Grainsberry and can't afford many resources.

OBJECT The first player who can make clothes, a meal, and a home wins.

→ CLOTHES = 🧶 + 🧵

→ MEAL = 🥕 + 🥩 + 🍼

→ SHELTER = 🧱 + ⚒️

SUPPLIES

game board *(next page)*
6 game tokens
 (a combination of buttons, paper clips, pebbles)
1 die *(6-sided)*
paper
pencil

DIRECTIONS

1. Scan and print the game board on the next page.

2. Distribute the six game tokens evenly, making sure each player gets all one type of token. For example, if you're playing with two players, player 1 should get three buttons and player 2 should get three pebbles. If you're playing with three players, player 1 should get two buttons, player 2 should get two paper clips, and player 3 should get two pebbles.

3. Roll the die; highest roller goes first. Player 1 puts a game token on the board in any space. Player 2 then puts one token in a different space. Take turns until all six spaces contain only one token each.

4. On your turn, roll the die. The space on the board that matches the die gives a resource only to the player who has a token there. For example: you roll a 3, which matches the die in the "eggs" space. Player 2 has a token there, so he or she gets money (since his or her make-believe family sells eggs). Player 2 writes "money" on his or her resource list.

5. The next player takes a turn, repeating step 2. On spaces that give more than one type of resource, pick only one and write it on your list.

6. Take turns rolling to gain resources. The pictures on this page show which resources you need to make a meal, clothes, and a shelter. On your turn, you can exchange any three resources for any one resource of your choice, or you can trade with other players who want to.

EXAMPLES: To make clothes, you need one wool and one thread, but you have no thread. You do have two milk and two wool. To exchange, cross out two milk and one wool on your score sheet and add one thread. To trade, ask if another player will give you one thread if you give one wool. Mark the trade on your score sheet. You can now make clothes.

GARDEN
vegetable

GIVE

COW
milk/meat

GIVE

EGGS
money

GIVE

CROPS
thread/vegetable

GIVE

TREES
building supplies

GIVE

CROPS
milk/wool

GIVE

ON THE PATH TO A FULL MEAL

Many problems keep kids from getting a full meal each day. See if you can help the children in the maze avoid some of the most common problems so they can make it to the nutritious food.

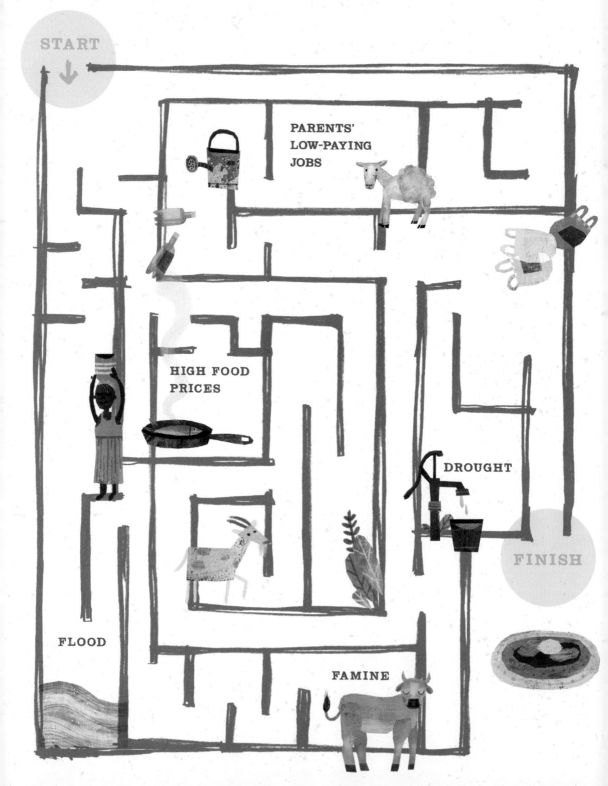

START

PARENTS' LOW-PAYING JOBS

HIGH FOOD PRICES

DROUGHT

FINISH

FLOOD

FAMINE

HUNGRY FOR MORE

Do you know the table manners and types of food from these countries?
Draw lines to connect the eating style to the country.

Never touch your food. Use your fork and knife to eat your meals—even pizza!

PHILIPPINES

Start your meal with a ball of fufu (like bread pudding) and tear off pieces to scoop up a spicy stew!

BRAZIL

Corn is ground up to make a dough called *masa*, which is part of just about every meal.

GHANA

Breakfast is not Cocoa Krispies, but chocolate rice porridge with a side of dried salty fish.

THAILAND

Eat your rice with a spoon! You can use the back side of your fork to push rice and meat and vegetables into the spoon.

MEXICO

Brazil=Never touch your food; Ghana=Start your meal with fufu; Mexico=Corn is ground to make a dough called masa; Philippines=Breakfast is not Cocoa Krispies; Thailand=Eat your rice with your spoon.

ACTION STEPS

1. SPONSOR A "BEANS AND RICE" LUNCH at your school or church. Charge five dollars for tickets. Show a map of countries where kids eat rice and beans, and give the money you raise to hungry kids in those countries. Below, record how much money you raised, which organization you sent it to, and how it will help the kids who receive it.

_____

_____

_____

_____

_____

_____

2. WITH AN ADULT, go to the recipes section at the end of this book (starting on p. 85) to find foods from around the world. Choose a recipe to make with your family. Research the country the food comes from and write what you learned on the lines below. Share the information with your family when you sit down to eat.

_____

_____

_____

_____

_____

PART 4

School

LEARNING AROUND THE WORLD

✕

I applied my mind
to study and to
explore by wisdom
all that is done
under the heavens.

ECCLESIASTES 1:13

PART 4
School

LEARNING AROUND THE WORLD

There is so much to learn about our world! God made this world full of such a variety of different people, plants, animals, and places, and it's fun to discover more about His creation. We can be grateful for the opportunity we have to go to school and learn from teachers and parents in subjects like science, math, language, and history.

The activities in this section will help you discover how children in the developing world learn. For example, as you play the bottle cap memory game, you can find out about children who work alongside their parents every day in giant garbage dumps. These children sift through the trash to find bottles and cans that can be recycled to earn some money. They also find creative ways to make toys out of recyclables.

You can also make a chalkboard with recycled materials. As you assemble it, you can think about children in the developing world who only use slates and chalk to study since they can't afford pencils and paper.

The most important thing we can learn about is God's truth and the way He loves us. That's the best education of all! Pray that God would give you wisdom to know how to pray for and help others who don't have as much as you do.

CRAFTS AND ACTIVITIES

BOTTLE CAP MEMORY GAME

Your mind can grow and learn in school, but did you know you can stretch your brain through games, too? Some children in developing countries don't have the chance to buy games and toys, so instead they collect items to make their own games. You can make your own game too!

+ Supplies

- 16 plastic bottle caps, all the same color (don't use clear caps)
- glue
- 4 small stones
- a handful of dirt (or sand)
- 4 small leaves
- 4 small twigs

= Directions

Apply glue to the inside of each bottle cap. Fill four caps with stones, four caps with dirt, four caps with leaves, and four caps with twigs. Allow the glue to dry.

HOW TO PLAY THE GAME

Turn the caps over so you can't see what's inside. Mix them up and spread them out, making four rows with four caps in each row. When it's your turn, turn over two caps. If they match, leave them turned over and pick two more to turn over. If they don't match, turn them back over and let your opponent take a turn. The first person to get four matching bottle caps turned over is the winner!

A BASKET FOR GOODIES

You can weave a basket to hold school supplies, just like some kids in other countries do.

✛ Supplies

- empty plastic water bottle (16 ounces)
- scissors
- 1 empty cereal box
- ruler
- pencil
- tape
- 1 rubber band

☰ Directions

1. Cut away the top third of the bottle so it measures about 4 inches tall.
2. Unfold the flaps of the cereal box at the top and bottom so the box lays flat. Then cut away the flaps and the sides. Your cardboard should be about 11 inches long.
3. Using a ruler and a pencil, mark every ½ inch from one of the long edges across to the other side. Then cut the cardboard into about 15 strips.
4. To make the base of the basket, lay two strips of cardboard on the table to form a plus sign. Secure them in the center with a small piece of tape. Add six more strips, taping each one and spacing them evenly to make a starburst.
5. With the printed side of the cereal box facing down, set the water bottle base on the center of the starburst and gently gather the strips up the sides of the water bottle. Place a rubber band around the top of the bottle to hold the strips in place.
6. Starting at the base, place a strip under another strip, and tape it in place. Then weave the strip over the next one and behind the next. Keep doing this all the way back to where you began. Trim the strip and secure it with tape.
7. Continue weaving rows of the strips until you reach the desired height. (If necessary, cut additional strips from the back of the cereal box.)
8. Using scissors, trim all the strips until they're level with the top of the basket. Fold the tape lengthwise and place it over the rim so it covers the inside and outside.
9. Remove the bottle or trim the bottle so it fits inside the basket and is out of view. Now your basket can hold pencils or anything else you'd like!

CHALKBOARD BOX

Most kids in developing countries use chalk and chalkboards for their classwork since paper is often too expensive. (Be sure to ask an adult for help with this activity.)

✚ Supplies

- disposable gloves (rubber or latex)
- a recycled shoebox or other box of similar size
- chalkboard paint (you can find some at your local craft store)
- paintbrush
- nontoxic chalk
- stickers, magazine pictures, photos, and other items to decorate your box
- chalkboard eraser or soft rag

▬ Directions

1. Outside or in a well-ventilated area, create a work space for painting. Be sure to wear rubber or latex gloves.
3. Paint the box and the lid with the chalkboard paint. Let it dry.
4. Apply a second coat, and let it dry.
5. Rub the dry, painted surface with white chalk to condition the chalkboard.
6. Erase the chalk.
7. Decorate the box with stickers, magazine pictures, or photos to make it your own.
8. Fill your box with school supplies. Don't forget to write on the lid of the box with the chalk!

BUILD YOUR OWN LUNCH BAG

Many poor families in Indonesia and the Philippines recycle juice boxes to make bright, fun bags like this one. They sell the bags to make money to feed their families. You can make a cool lunch bag too!

✚ Supplies

- 16 empty, clean juice pouches (such as Capri Sun), with the tops cut off
- 1 roll of brightly colored duct tape (you can find this at your local craft store)
- scissors
- 20-inch strip of sturdy ribbon (2 inches wide)

☰ Directions

1. Cut the pouches apart, separating the fronts and the backs.
2. To make the front of your bag, lay four pouch pieces face down to form two rows. Tape the pieces together. Repeat with four more pouch pieces for the back.
3. To make the sides and the bottom of the bag, tape two pouch pieces together. Repeat this two more times so you have three identical pieces.
4. Place the taped two-piece panels face down next to each other in a straight line. Cover each seam with tape.
5. Turn over the taped panel line so it's face up. Overlap the open edges of each end to form the bag. Tape this seam together on the inside of the bag. It will look like a tube.
6. Insert the last taped piece to create the bottom of the bag. Using smaller pieces of tape (3 to 4 inches long), tape the bottom piece to the formed bag from the inside. To make the bottom of the bag stronger, tape the longer pieces of tape on the outside of the bag too.

7. To make the handle, tape each end of the ribbon inside the bag on each side. Use more tape to cover each end of the handle inside the bag so it's strong enough to hold your yummy lunch!

Here's another fun idea—you can make another bag for a friend and fill it up with his or her favorite healthy treats!

KEEPSAKE BOX

Children in developing countries sometimes make their own containers for their favorite items. Do you have some artwork, pictures, or school papers you want to keep safe? Find a place for them with this fun project!

Supplies

- pie tin or other shallow dish
- 1 cup clear-drying craft glue
- ½ cup water
- 1 clean pizza box or any wide, shallow box
- wrapping paper
- glue
- colored duct tape
- safety scissors
- magazine pages, comics, or brightly colored paper
- paintbrush

Directions

1. In the pie tin, mix the water and the craft glue. Set aside.
2. Line the outside and inside of the box with wrapping paper and glue it in. The box should be covered completely.
3. Reinforce the box corners with duct tape.
4. Cut out pictures to decorate the top and bottom of the box.
5. Dip the cutout designs in the glue mixture.
6. Press the designs on top of the box lid and let it dry.
7. Paint the outside of the box with an extra coat of glue. Let it dry.
8. Place your keepsakes in the box and store it under your dresser, desk, or bed.

You can also make more than one box and give them to grandparents or other family members.

ALANYU'S SCHOOL DAY

Use the word bank below to fill in the blanks about a day in the life of Alanyu, a 10-year-old student in East Africa.

WORD BANK

Luganda
uniform
porridge
textbook

homework
stream
Nyaga Nyaga Nya
garden

ALANYU is 10 years old and lives in Uganda. He wakes up very early to get to school on time. It's still dark outside when he washes his face with water from a nearby _____. He eats a breakfast _____ and gets dressed in his _____. He walks many miles to the small schoolhouse. There are many students of different ages in his class. His first lesson of the day is _____,

the study of his local language. When it's time for lunch, Alanyu sometimes doesn't eat, because meals cost extra money. When his parents can afford to buy him lunch, he eats a meal called posho, a dish made of corn and beans. At recess, Alanyu plays a game with his friends called _____. It is a lot like Duck, Duck, Goose. He often has to share a _____ with other students, because they also cost extra money.

When classes end, the students clean the classroom and work in the school's vegetable _____. It is very late by the time Alanyu arrives back home. He finishes his _____ just in time for bed.

SCHOOL FACTS

UGANDA
THAILAND
HAITI
KENYA
BRAZIL

In this country, students learn as many as 10 subjects and attend school for up to 12 hours in one day.

1

Since an earthquake ruined many of the schools in this country, most children here attend class in tents.

2

In this country, kids have a quiet hour at school for meditating and saying prayers.

3

In this country, a principal is called a headmaster.

4

Instead of receiving letter grades, children in this country are graded on a scale from 0 to10.

5

1. Kenya
2. Haiti
3. Thailand
4. Uganda
5. Brazil

FIND THE FLAG

How many flags of other countries can you recognize?

1.

2.

3.

4.

KENYA
THAILAND
BRAZIL
MEXICO
UGANDA
RWANDA
PERU
HAITI

5.

6.

7.

8.

1. Thailand; 2. Peru; 3. Uganda; 4. Haiti; 5. Rwanda; 6. Kenya; 7. Brazil; 8. Mexico

QUIZ: WHAT KIND OF JOB FITS YOU?

Poverty makes it tough for people to reach their goals, which is why it's so important for children to have hope, a plan for their future, and educational opportunities. Think about your own hopes and dreams while you take this quiz.

1. You feel bored, so you
   a. play hospital with your stuffed animals.
   b. put together a jigsaw puzzle.
   c. call a friend on the phone.
   d. redecorate your bedroom.
   e. take your dog for a walk.

2. Your ideal role in the Christmas play would be to
   a. guide audience members to their seats.
   b. build the props and scenes for the play.
   c. star as Joseph or Mary.
   d. write lines for the actors to say.
   e. train the animal actors.

3. You'd love to take a trip to
   a. an orphanage to cook and clean for kids.
   b. Space Camp to float in the zero-gravity room.
   c. Peru to learn the Spanish language.
   d. the School of Rock to play the guitar.
   e. the Rocky Mountains to camp and explore.

4. For a class project, you choose to research
   a. how penicillin cures sickness.
   b. the history of Egyptian mummies.
   c. the best speeches ever given.
   d. famous artists or musicians.
   e. plants that eat insects.

5. You'd enjoy watching a movie about
   a. a kid trying to make friends in a new town.
   b. robots taking over the world.
   c. someone who made a difference in the world by speaking out.
   d. a closet that leads to a magical land.
   e. a cat that gets lost in the woods.

6. Your parents or friends describe you as
   a. generous.
   b. curious.
   c. social.
   d. artistic.
   e. outdoorsy.

Add up your score by totaling the number of letters you chose for each question. Look at the results below, and then research these professions.

MOSTLY A'S
You love helping people, so a job as a doctor, teacher, pastor, firefighter, or counselor may be a great fit for you.

MOSTLY B'S
You're a problem solver, so you may make a great astronaut, chemist, financial planner, engineer, or pilot.

MOSTLY C'S
Communicating is your strong suit. Consider a job as a journalist, marketer, performer, lawmaker, or diplomat.

MOSTLY D'S
With your creative spirit, you'd likely do well as a musician, designer, chef, artist, or filmmaker.

MOSTLY E'S
You connect well with God's creation, so you could make a great veterinarian, landscaper, farmer, park ranger, or botanist.

GOAL

Praying

Dropping out
of school

Training &
studying

Going to
church

Having
faith

Feeling
hopeless

HELP

Getting
help

Joining
a gang

Doing
it alone

Working
a job

Going to
school

START

CHASING THE DREAM
Help Adriana choose the chickens that take the
best paths to the top of the mountain.

♀♀ ACTION STEPS

1. Many school children in Africa have never owned a book. Go through your books to see if there are some you can give away. With your parents, organize a book sale and donate the money you raise to a ministry that provides educational resources for people in need. Write down how much you raised, who you gave it to, and anything else you want to remember about the experience.

_____

_____

_____

_____

_____

_____

2. Many students who live in poverty can't afford school supplies or school uniforms, which means they can't go to school. Other kids have to work instead of going to school. Read Proverbs 19:17, and think of some ways you can help raise funds for children's school supplies. Write your ideas here:

_____

_____

_____

_____

_____

_____

_____

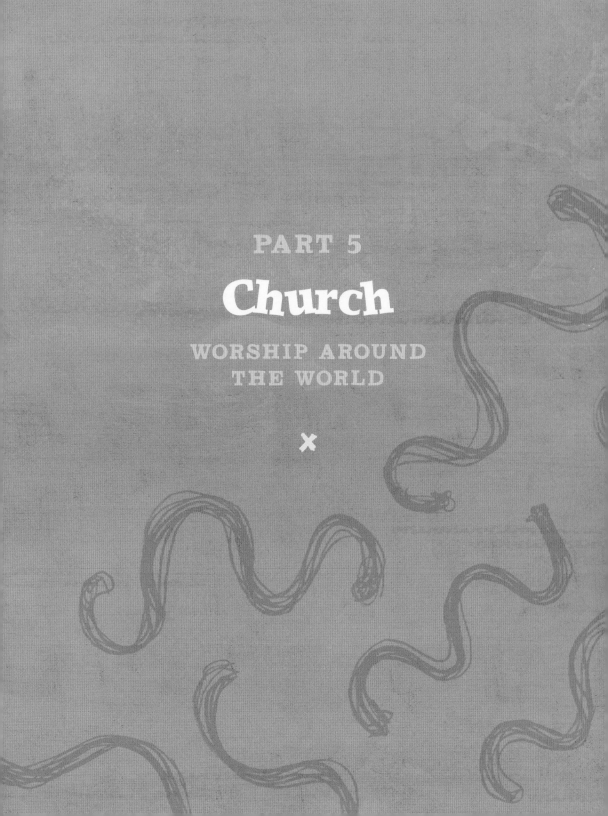

PART 5

Church

WORSHIP AROUND
THE WORLD

✕

**The nations
will praise you for
ever and ever.**

PSALM 45:17

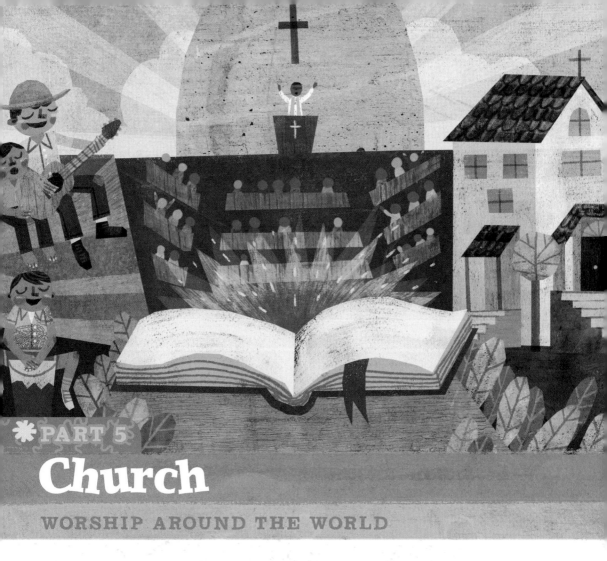

Church

WORSHIP AROUND THE WORLD

If you traveled all around the world going to different churches, you'd find lots of different kinds of services. Children from some congregations use books to sing and pray. Some sit outside under a big tree for church. But no matter how different our churches are, children everywhere love to praise God and pray for one another!

The activities in this section will help you learn about God's love for children all over the world. God invites you to love and pray for children who are like you but who don't have enough money for basic needs such as food, clean water, and medicine.

For example, the "Leaf a Message" activity is a fun way to remind you to pray for others. And the "Walking in Wisdom Maze" is an activity you can do with a friend. As you look up the Scripture verses and talk about them, you can be thankful for the Bible and the way God leads us.

The activities in this section help us think about people who worship God all over the world. Imagine the smile on God's face when He hears prayers and singing in thousands of different languages! Remember to pray that everyone in the world will know Jesus and His great love.

CRAFTS AND ACTIVITIES

A PUZZLE WITH A PURPOSE

Create a puzzle that features your own artwork and a Bible verse about friendship. Use a rubber band to hold the puzzle together, and give it to a friend as a fun gift!

✚ Supplies

- 8–10 wooden sticks from Popsicles or a craft store
- masking tape
- markers
- a Bible verse about friendship or kindness (see examples below)

≡ Directions

1. Line up the sticks lengthwise so no gaps show between. Put two strips of masking tape across them.
2. Flip over the cluster of sticks and use a marker to write a Bible reference across the sticks. You can choose one of the verses about friendship and kindness below, or you can read the Bible to find a different verse.
3. Using markers, draw a colorful picture on the sticks. Make sure every stick has some color on it.
4. Flip over the cluster of sticks and remove the tape.
5. Turn the sticks over again and shuffle them. Now try to put your puzzle back together!

BIBLE VERSES

Dear friends, let us love one another, for love comes from God.
1 JOHN 4:7

A friend is always loyal, and a brother is born to help in time of need.
PROVERBS 17:17, NLT

Be devoted to one another in love. Honor one another above yourselves.
ROMANS 12:10

FRUITY FUN BOOKMARKS

The Bible talks about the fruit of the Spirit—the traits God produces in us as we become more like Him. These include love, joy, peace, patience, kindness, goodness, faithfulness, gentleness, and self-control (see Galatians 5:22-23). Here's how you can make a fun bookmark that reminds you of the fruit of the Spirit!

╋ Supplies

- colored construction paper
- pencil
- safety scissors
- colored markers
- 1 laminating sheet or clear contact paper

═ Directions

1. Trace a fruit shape (such as an apple, a banana, or an orange) on construction paper. Cut out the shape.
2. Write these words on your bookmark: My prayer for _____ [insert the name of the person you want to pray for] is _____ [insert what you are praying for them).
3. Decorate the rest of the bookmark with colorful designs or stickers.
4. Laminate the bookmark or cover it with clear contact paper, trimming off any extra around the edges.
5. Give the bookmark to the person you are praying for.

No matter where you go to church, one of the important parts of worship is thanking God for all He has done for us. But you don't have to be in church to have a grateful heart! After you make this book, you can add an idea or picture each day about the ways God provides for you.

➕ Supplies

- hole punch
- 2 pieces of cardboard, each cut into the shape of a 4-by-6-inch bread slice
- pencil
- 5 pieces of paper, each cut into the shape of a 4-by-6-inch bread slice
- safety scissors
- ruler
- yarn, ribbon, or metal rings
- markers, crayons, or colored pencils

➖ Directions

1. Using the hole punch, make two holes on the top of the cardboard bread slices. The holes should be three to four inches apart. (These pieces of cardboard will be the front and back of the book.)
2. Repeat the hole punches on the five pieces of paper so the holes all line up. (These will be the inside pages.)
3. Fasten the front cover, inside pages, and back cover together with a piece of yarn, ribbon, or metal rings.
4. Decorate the front and back of the book with markers, crayons, or colored pencils.
5. On the inside pages, draw pictures or write words to show what you're thankful for!

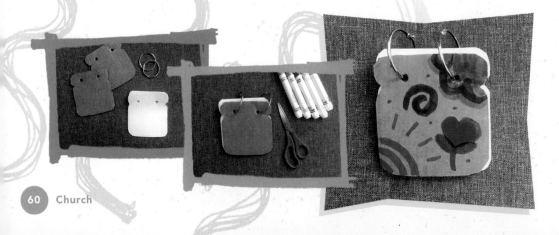

GRATITUDE ROCKS!

Did you know that a simple rock can remind you to be thankful? After the Lord protected the Israelites from their enemies, Samuel took a large stone and placed it between two towns. He nicknamed the stone "the stone of help," because it was a reminder to the people that the Lord had helped them (see 1 Samuel 7:12).

Paint some stones with pictures or words describing what you're grateful for. You can place them in a jar on your kitchen table, or you can also hide them and then search for them like it's an Easter egg hunt!

✚ Supplies

- colorful paint pens (such as Elmer's paint markers)
- several smooth, flat rocks

☰ Directions

1. Go hunting for rocks in your yard. Once you've collected several, rinse them well with water. Lay them out to dry.
2. On the first dry rock, write or draw something you're thankful for. Draw some fun designs and patterns. Be sure to wait for the first layer of paint to dry before adding other layers of color.
3. Repeat with all your rocks!

LEAF A MESSAGE

This tree with leaves can remind you to pray. Each day you can pull off a new leaf and say the prayer on it!

Supplies

- leaf templates (see p. 103)
- scissors
- pen or fine-tip marker
- glue
- 2–3 sheets of construction paper
- hole punch
- 6 or more twigs or thin branches (at least 2 feet long)
- 1 vase or jar (such as a big canning jar)
- several pieces of string (3–4 inches long)

Directions

1. Scan and print out the sheet of leaf templates.
2. Cut out each leaf.
3. Some leaves have prayers printed on them, while others are blank so you can fill in your own. On each blank leaf, write something you want to say to God or ask Him.
4. With a thin layer of glue, paste each leaf onto construction paper. Cut the construction paper in the shape of the leaves, leaving a ½-inch border of construction paper showing.
5. Punch a small hole near an edge of each leaf.
6. Place the branches inside the vase or jar. The jar should be tall enough to keep them propped up. If not, add stones or sand to the jar.
7. Lace the pieces of string through the leaves, and then tie them around the branches. Every day you can pull one off and say the prayer!

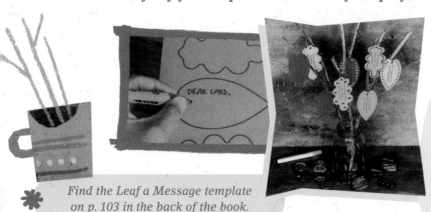

Find the Leaf a Message template on p. 103 in the back of the book.

ANOTHER OPTION: Instead of using the leaf template, you can cut out your own leaves from construction paper. Then write prayers on them with a marker and follow the rest of the steps.

MARCH TO YOUR OWN BEAT

In many African countries, musicians play a traditional drum called a *djembe* (JEM-bay). These drums are often played in church services to worship the Lord. Here's how to create your own drum so you can make a joyful noise too!

✚ Supplies

- 2 large paper cups
- packing tape
- 20–30 strips of newspaper
- paint
- paintbrush
- 1 balloon
- 1 rubber band
- 1 cup flour and 1 cup water, mixed together

⚌ Directions

1. Cut the bottom out of both cups. Place one cup upside down on table. Place the other cup right-side up on top of the other cup. Tape the two cups together.
2. Dip the strips of newspaper into the water and flour mixture, and wrap the strips around the cups. Put several layers around the top rim to make it stronger. Let it dry.
3. Use paint to decorate your drum in a colorful design.
4. Once the paint has dried, cut open one side of the balloon and stretch it over the top of the cup. Use a rubber band to secure it to the lid.
5. Play the drum with your hands while singing songs of worship to God.

ACTION STEPS

1. JESUS OFTEN SPOKE in parables, which are simple stories that have a deep meaning or spiritual lesson. Read Matthew 25:14-30, then discuss these questions:

What talents or gifts do you have that you could use to serve other people?

_____

_____

_____

_____

_____

_____

_____

How has someone else served you with their gifts or talents?

_____

_____

_____

_____

_____

_____

_____

2. JESUS IS CALLED the Bread of Life because everyone who believes in Him will be filled up spiritually. God wants to take care of all of our spiritual needs *and* our physical needs. Read Matthew 14:13-21, the story of Jesus feeding 5,000 people with only a few loaves of bread and a few fish. With your family or your Sunday school class, volunteer at a soup kitchen or another ministry in your community. Write about your experience here:

_____

_____

_____

_____

_____

_____

LIFE IN LIMA

Paola lives in Lima, the capital of the country of Peru in South America. Help her find her way from her home to Compassion's child development center, and see what you can learn along the way!

Machu Picchu

Andes Mountains

Paola's home (casa)

houses on steep hills

roofs made of a plastic sheet

no electricity in many homes

trash (basura)

cooking over an open fire

healthy food to eat

water truck delivering water to the people

church (iglesia)

A B C

school (escuela)

no running water or flush toilets

Compassion Student Center

WALKING IN WISDOM

One of the things we can learn from the Bible is how to make wise choices. Starting at the church, collect nuggets of wisdom from the Bible along the path. Then pass them along to a friend at the end!

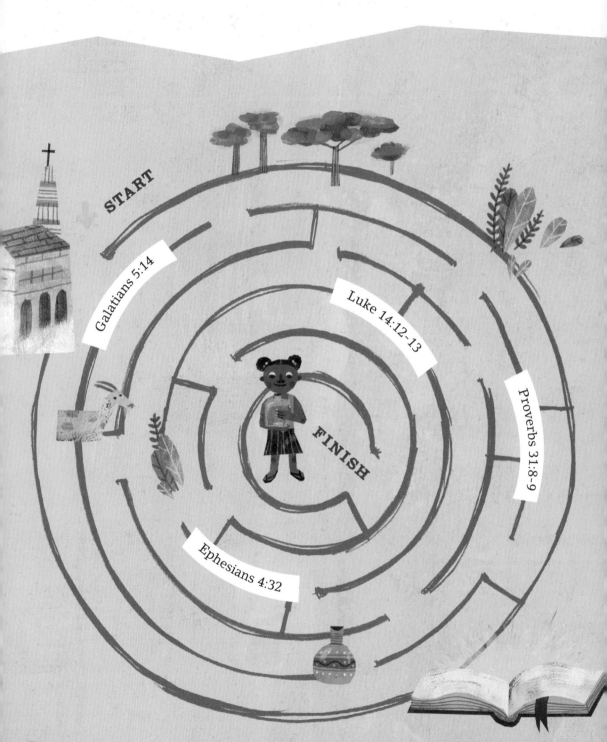

START

Galatians 5:14

Luke 14:12-13

Proverbs 31:8-9

FINISH

Ephesians 4:32

THE WAY OF RESPECT

The Bible tells us to show love and respect to others (see 1 Peter 2:17). Do you show respect to everyone? Take this quiz to find out.

1. A boy in a wheelchair is having trouble opening a door. What do you do?
   a. Say, "Let me help," roll his chair out of the way, and open the door for him.
   b. Ask him if he could use some help.
   c. Walk by, pretending not to notice.

2. A girl in your class doesn't celebrate birthdays, Easter, or Christmas. You ask why, and she tells you it's because of her family's religion. What do you do?
   a. Say, "That's just silly!"
   b. Ask her to eat lunch with you so you can learn more about each other's families and beliefs.
   c. Stop talking to her because you shouldn't be friends with people who have different beliefs.

3. Your friend told you he has a learning disability. At recess you hear a group of kids calling him mean names. What do you do?
   a. Stick up for your friend by shouting insults at the bullies.
   b. Take your friend by the hand and go play somewhere else.
   c. Stay out of the conflict completely.

4. You meet a new student who is blind. At recess, what do you do?
   a. Lead her around by the hand as much as possible.
   b. Let her be independent, treating her like you treat your other friends.
   c. Act embarrassed to be seen with her.

5. A boy who lives next door comes over and asks you to play outside. You know he doesn't speak much English. What do you do?
   a. Tell him you'll play with him after he learns better English.
   b. Grab your soccer ball and head outside. If you can't understand each other's words, you can try to communicate with actions.
   c. Tell him you can't play. You'd feel awkward if you couldn't understand him.

MOSTLY A'S: HEAVY-HANDED HELPER

You mean well, but you're too quick to jump in with assistance or opinions. Instead, get to know other kids and ask them questions before assuming you know what they need.

MOSTLY B'S: RESPECTFUL ALLY

You go out of your way to make everyone feel accepted. You enjoy finding out about people's families, talents, and cultures. You realize that people who are different from you are loved by God, just as you are.

MOSTLY C'S: HANDS-OFF HIDER

You're not sure how to act around people who are different from you, so you shy away. Try to focus on the things you have in common with others instead of the things that make you different. Speak up when you see something happening that's wrong.

PART 6

Clothing and Toys

FUN AROUND
THE WORLD

✕

My God will meet all your needs according to the riches of his glory in Christ Jesus.

PHILIPPIANS 4:19

Clothing and Toys

FUN AROUND THE WORLD

It's fun to find out what life is like for children all over the world! We can be inspired by the way other children work and play. The activities in this section will help you answer some questions such as "What do kids in other countries wear?" and "What do kids in other countries do for fun?"

Most of us don't think much about where we will find clothes to wear or what we can do to have fun. We just go to our closets or playrooms and find exactly what we need. Sometimes we even have a hard time choosing what outfit to wear or which toy we want to play with!

Children all over the world have fun even if they don't shop at toy stores and don't have much money to spend on toys and games. Many children in the developing world don't have many clothes to wear, and some make shoes out of materials other people throw away, like old tires. As you follow the instructions in the "Jump for Joy" activity, you can enjoy being creative and making something without spending any money.

One thing is true: no matter where we live and what we have, God knows what we need. As you pray for God to help the world's poorest children, remember that He can meet their needs—and ours, too!

CRAFTS AND ACTIVITIES

COCONUT RACERS!

In Thailand, kids play *dern kala*, a game where they walk on coconut shells. You can play too! Just follow the instructions below. (Be sure to ask an adult for help with this activity.)

+ Supplies

- 2 whole coconuts
- 1 kitchen knife
- 1 nail
- 5 feet of thick string

Directions

1. Ask an adult to use the blunt side of a kitchen knife to tap the seams of the coconuts until they split open.
2. Scrape out the coconut.
3. Use a nail to make a hole at the top of each shell.
4. Pull one end of the string through the hole of one shell. Then pull the other end through the hole on the other shell.
5. Tie a large knot at the ends of the string to hold it in place when pulled.
6. Place one foot on the outside of each shell, grab the string, and race away!

MANCALA

Mancala (pronounced mahn-CAH-lah) is a simple game of strategy that goes back thousands of years. Since this game is played all over the world, there are more than 400 ways to play it!

Supplies

- 1 empty egg carton
- 2 small empty bowls
- 48 small stones, beads, buttons, or marbles

Directions

Put four stones in each egg cup of the carton. Place the carton on a flat surface between two players, and put one bowl at each end of the carton. The object is to collect the most stones in your bowl.

HOW TO PLAY THE GAME

Each player controls the cups closest to them and the bowls to their right. To start your turn, scoop up the four stones from any one of your cups. Drop one stone into the cup on the right of the starting cup and continue to the right, dropping one stone in each cup. When you come to your bowl on the right end, drop a stone into the bowl and continue dropping one stone per cup on the other side of the board, going counterclockwise, until you have no more stones in your hand. If you put the last stone into an empty cup when it's your turn, you get to capture all the stones in the cup directly across from it on your opponent's side. Player 2 does the same with all the stones from one of their cups. Continue taking turns until all the cups are empty. Whoever has the most stones wins!

OSSELETS

The game of osselets (pronounced oss-LAY) is like the game of jacks, but some children in Haiti play it with the knuckle bones of goats—no kidding! The word *osselets* means "small bones" in French, a language that is widely spoken in Haiti.

Supplies

1 package of colored modeling clay
colorful paint
1 small ball

Directions

1. Make five cubes (½-inch each) out of modeling clay. Each cube should be a different color.
2. Using a contrasting color of paint, place one dot on each cube. Let them dry.

HOW TO PLAY THE GAME

The first player begins by gently tossing all five osselets (dice) into the air and letting them land on the ground. The player then picks up the ball, tosses it in the air, and tries to pick up one of the dice before the ball hits the ground. The goal is for the player to pick up an extra osselet each time until they have all five in hand.

Here's the tricky part: before the player can pick up the osselet, they have to turn it so the side with only one dot is facing up. If an osselet falls on the ground before another is picked up, it's the next player's turn.

GROCERY BAG BALLS

Some kids in Africa can't afford to buy toys, so they make them. See if you can make a ball too! (Be sure to ask an adult for help with this activity.)

Supplies

- 6 plastic shopping bags (grocery size)
- yarn or twine

Directions

1. Wad five bags into a ball.
2. Place the wad of bags into another bag.
3. Wrap the handles of the bag around the wad and tie the ends together.
4. Wrap the twine or yarn around the ball and tie the ends. You are now ready for a game of soccer!

Reusing items helps keep trash out of landfills and oceans. And since kids living in poverty don't have extra money for toys, they often make toys by reusing old items. You can reuse plastic bags to make a jump rope!

Supplies

- 6–8 plastic grocery bags
- scissors
- masking tape
- duct tape

Directions

1. Lay one bag flat and fold it in half lengthwise. Fold it in half again.
2. Cut off and discard the bag's bottom and handles. Then cut across the bag to make sections about one inch across. Repeat this with each of the bags. When you unfold the sections, you will get loops.
3. Knot two of the loops together with a "strap hitch" by pulling an end of loop 1 under and up through loop 2, then back through loop 1. Then pull both loops outward to form a knot. Keep attaching loops this way until your strand is about 10 feet long.
4. Repeat step 3 to make six more strands.
5. Tie together three strands at the top. Attach the knotted end to a secure surface with masking or duct tape. Braid the three strands, tying a knot at the end.
6. Repeat step 5 with the other three strands. Then twist together both thick strands into one jump rope. Wrap duct tape around the edges to form handles.

All kids need comfortable shoes to protect their feet from sharp objects on the ground. As you make these silly shoes out of empty tissue boxes, imagine how it would feel to wear shoes as uncomfortable as these all the time. Pray for kids who don't have safe shoes.

✚ Supplies

- 2 empty tissue boxes (rectangular)
- acrylic paint
- 1 paintbrush
- pen
- 2 shoelaces (or 12-inch-long pieces of sturdy string)

▤ Directions

1. Paint the tissue boxes to look like a pair of shoes. Let the paint dry.
2. With a pen, make three dots on each side of the hole in the box to show where the shoelace holes will go. Then poke the pen through to make the holes.
3. Lace the boxes like you would with regular shoes. Then put your feet inside and tie up your laces.

PUZZLES

HEART AND SOLES

What are your favorite shoes to wear? Follow this maze to find out why shoes are extra important for children living in poverty.

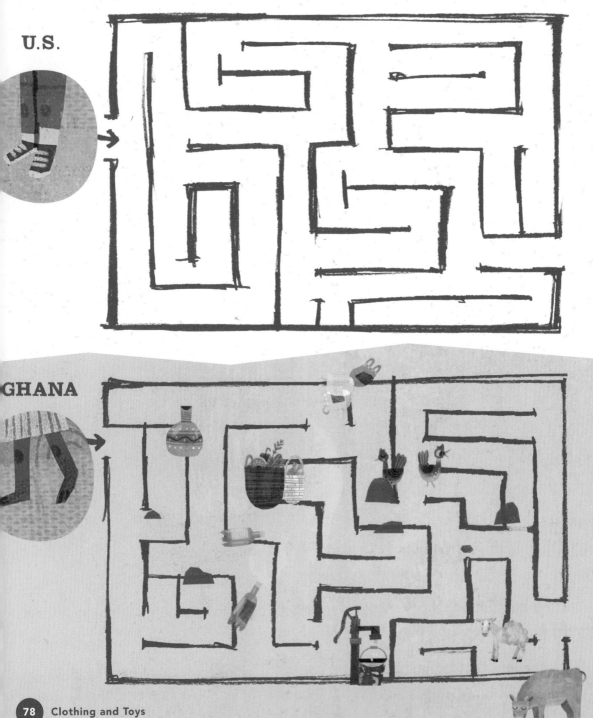

U.S.

GHANA

TOY HUNT

Children living in poverty have to be creative to make toys that don't cost money. They use materials they find around their homes and streets. Help Jean collect items on his walk home from his school in Haiti. Then see what toys he can make out of them!

empty plastic soda bottles

cooking-oil can

ears of corn

wooden board

string/twine

several grocery bags

pieces of paper

Check out the types of toys Jean can make with the items he collected!

SOCCER BALL

PAPER BEADS

GUITAR

CORN-HUSK DOLL

SODA BOTTLE CAR

FUN FACTS ABOUT SHOES

The oldest known leather shoe is 5,500 years old.

High heels originated in Turkey in the 1400s.

Ballerinas wear "pointe shoes" to protect their feet when they're dancing on their tiptoes.

In Africa and Asia, children walk an average of 3.7 miles a day just to fetch water.

In some parts of Ethiopia, kids walk more than 12 miles to just get to school!

MAKE A RUN FOR IT!

Can you spot the 14 differences between these two scenes?

Running is a popular sport in Kenya. Long-distance runners from Kenya are considered the best in the world and win many medals in the Olympics and other competitions. Having a race is a way to have fun with friends—and it doesn't cost anything!

_____   _____
_____   _____
_____   _____
_____   _____
_____   _____
_____   _____
_____   _____

See answers on following page (p. 82)

1. Find a running-shoe store in your community that could help send shoes to poor areas around the world. Then host a shoe drive to collect new or gently used tennis shoes from family members and friends. Write down how many shoes you collected and where they were sent:

_____

_____

_____

_____

_____

2. Go through your toys and games and see if there are some you can get rid of. Then have a garage sale and give the money to an organization that helps kids who don't have toys. Write down the organization you gave to and why you picked that one:

_____

_____

_____

_____

Answer key: "Make A Run For It" (p. 80-81)

RECIPES

COOKING AROUND THE WORLD

Do you have any favorite family recipes or meals that you like to eat at holidays? Food plays an important role in building traditions, memories, and cultures. No matter where we live, meals are a meaningful way to spend time together thanking God for His blessings and strengthening our relationships with family and friends.

The recipes in this section are broken down by continent to give you an idea of what people around the world eat. Try making and eating them with your family and friends—you might even make some new traditions and memories as you do!

East African Chapati

Chapati is a thin, round flatbread often eaten in East Africa. Children in Rwanda enjoy it as a snack with milk or tea, or as a meal with stew.

INGREDIENTS

2 cups flour

½ teaspoon salt

1 tablespoon plus 2 teaspoons vegetable oil

¼ cup water plus additional as needed

1 tablespoon shortening or cooking oil

DIRECTIONS

1. Mix flour and salt. Add the 1 tablespoon vegetable oil, and mix with your hands.
2. Slowly add water and knead in, adding more as needed until an elastic (stretchy) dough is formed.
3. Divide dough into four equal parts. With your hand, flatten one ball into a circle on a lightly floured surface and spread ½ teaspoon of the oil over it. Roll it up like a jelly roll, then roll it up again so it resembles a snail shell. Repeat for each piece.
4. Let dough balls sit at least 20 minutes, or up to 8 hours.
5. With lightly floured rolling pin, flatten balls into 10-inch circles.
6. Heat shortening in a frying pan, then add a dough circle. Fry, turning once, until each side is golden brown and spotted. Dough will bubble as it fries. Repeat for each flatbread.

Makes 4 flatbreads.

Golden Couscous

Couscous is a popular food in Africa. Some history experts believe that people have been cooking this grain since before the tenth century in the parts of Africa now called Burkina Faso and Ghana.

INGREDIENTS

6 cups vegetable broth or chicken broth
6 tablespoons butter
3 cups chopped onions (4 to 5 medium onions)
2 teaspoons ground turmeric
1 teaspoon ground cumin
3 cups couscous (about 1 pound)
salt and pepper, to taste
2/3 cup slivered almonds, toasted (optional)

DIRECTIONS

1. Bring broth to a boil in a medium-size saucepan. Reduce heat to very low and cover.

2. Melt butter in a large saucepan over medium heat. Add onions and sauté until tender and light golden, about 8 minutes. Add turmeric and cumin. Stir 1 minute.

3. Add couscous to onion mixture and stir until coated. Mix in hot broth, then remove from heat. Cover and let stand until broth is absorbed, about 12 minutes.

4. Fluff couscous with a fork and season with salt and pepper. Place on a plate and sprinkle with almonds if using.

Makes 8 servings.

West African Peanut Soup

Many people throughout West Africa enjoy cooking soup made with groundnuts, which is another name for peanuts. Kids love it too! This creamy, hearty stew helps keep many kids' bellies full! Try it with your favorite toppings, like sour cream or chives.

INGREDIENTS

3 tablespoons vegetable oil
1 cup chopped onion (1 to 2 medium onions)
4 garlic cloves, minced
1 tablespoon minced fresh ginger
1 tablespoon curry powder
1 can (14 ounces) diced tomatoes
3 ½ cups chicken broth or vegetable broth
½ cup peanut butter
1 cup cubed sweet potatoes (1 to 2 medium sweet potatoes)
2 cups sliced okra (about ½ pound)
1 cup chopped green beans (about ⅓ pound)
chopped peanuts for garnish
salt and pepper, to taste

DIRECTIONS

1. Heat oil in a skillet and cook onion until soft, about 5 minutes. Add garlic, ginger, and curry powder and cook for several minutes just until hot, making sure garlic does not burn.
2. Add tomatoes, broth, and peanut butter. Bring to a boil and cook for about 10 minutes.
3. Add sweet potatoes, okra, and green beans and cook for about 15 more minutes, or until vegetables are tender.
4. Ladle into bowls and sprinkle with peanuts, salt, and pepper.

Makes 4 servings.

Khao Ber

In Thailand kids help gather vegetables from their families' gardens or buy vegetables to make this delicious soup. If their parents can afford it, they add pork too.

INGREDIENTS

8 cups water

3 cups rice

1 pound pork, cut into small chunks

2 small chili peppers, minced

2 to 3 cups of vegetables, such as string beans or mushrooms

3 cloves garlic, minced

salt to taste

DIRECTIONS

1. Bring water to a boil in a large pot. Add rice and boil until cooked, about 20 to 30 minutes.
2. Add the pork to the pot, followed by the chili peppers, vegetables, garlic, and salt. Boil until pork is done and mixture becomes thick, about 7 minutes.

Makes 4 servings.

After-School Snack Mix

Many kids living in poverty don't eat snacks after school because their families don't even have enough food for breakfast, lunch, and dinner. But Compassion student centers provide snacks or meals for kids, like this one from a center in Bangladesh. Give it a try and see what you think!

INGREDIENTS

1 medium onion, finely chopped
1 medium potato, boiled and diced
½ cup diced cucumber (about ½ small cucumber)
¼ cup chickpeas, boiled
4 teaspoons lemon juice (about 1 small lemon)
2 ½ teaspoons masala powder or curry powder
¼ cup roasted peanuts
2 tablespoons shredded coconut
salt to taste
2 teaspoons mustard oil (optional)
2 cups puffed rice cereal

DIRECTIONS

1. Mix the onion, potato, cucumber, chickpeas, lemon juice, masala powder, peanuts, coconut, salt, and mustard oil (if using) together in a large bowl.
2. Gently mix in the puffed rice.
3. Serve and enjoy as an after-school snack.

Makes 6 servings.

Thai Sticky Rice

Rice is the main food for half the population of the world. People in Asia grow and eat the most rice. In Asia, rice is also used to make paper, rope, packing material, and even toothpaste! In Thailand, sticky rice is a special treat often served at parties. Grab a pot and invite some friends—it's time to celebrate!

INGREDIENTS

2 cups sweet rice, uncooked (also called glutinous rice or sticky rice)
3½ cups water
1 teaspoon salt
2 tablespoons brown sugar
1 cup coconut milk
2 tablespoons toasted sesame seeds
1 fresh mango, chopped, or 1 cup frozen mango chunks, thawed

DIRECTIONS

1. Place the rice in a pot and pour water over it. Let it soak for 1 hour.
2. Add salt to the rice and cook on high until it boils.
3. Reduce the heat to low and partially cover the pot with a lid. Cook about 10 to 20 minutes, until the water is absorbed and the rice is soft. Set aside.
4. Pour the coconut milk into a pot and bring it to a boil.
5. Add the brown sugar and stir thoroughly.
6. Remove from heat and pour the mixture over the sticky rice.
7. Put some rice on a plate, sprinkle with sesame seeds, and add some mango. Then dig in!

Makes 4 servings.

Besitos de Coco

Besitos de coco (coconut kisses) are a favorite treat in the Spanish-speaking Caribbean islands, such as the Dominican Republic and Puerto Rico.

INGREDIENTS

2 tablespoons butter, softened

1 cup brown sugar

4 egg yolks

2 teaspoons coconut extract (or vanilla extract)

½ cup flour

3 cups coconut flakes

melted chocolate (optional)

DIRECTIONS

1. Preheat the oven to 350 degrees.
2. Grease two cookie sheets.
3. Cream together the butter and brown sugar, then mix in the egg yolks and coconut extract.
4. Mix in the flour. Stir in coconut flakes until a soft dough is formed.
5. Divide the dough into 24 balls.
6. Place the balls on the cookie sheets and bake for about 20 minutes or until golden. Share some with a friend!

Makes 24 cookies.

Saucy Chicken

Chicken is a common food in Haiti for families who can afford it. Many of the poorest people in Haiti can't afford to buy meat. Serve this chicken dish with a bowl of white rice and red beans.

INGREDIENTS

6 boneless chicken thighs
1 lemon, cut in half
salt and pepper to taste
4–5 tablespoons oil
1 large onion, chopped
1 large green pepper, chopped
2 cloves garlic, chopped
1 can (8 ounces) tomato paste
¾ cup water
1 teaspoon ground cloves

DIRECTIONS

1. Rub the chicken thighs with the lemon halves, squeezing out the juice as you rub. Sprinkle both sides of the chicken with salt and pepper.
2. Heat the oil in a pan on medium high, and fry the chicken thighs on each side, just until browned.
3. Lay the chicken pieces in a baking pan and cover them with the onion and green pepper.
4. In a small bowl, whisk the garlic, tomato paste, water, and ground cloves. Pour the sauce over chicken.
5. Bake at 350 degrees, uncovered, for about 45 minutes, or until the chicken is fully cooked.

Makes 4–6 servings.

White Bean and Chorizo Stew

This spicy stew is popular in the Dominican Republic, where people often serve it with white rice.

INGREDIENTS
2 tablespoons olive oil
1 pound spicy chorizo, sliced (you can also use a mild or sweet sausage if you don't like spicy food)
1 medium red onion, diced
4 cloves garlic, crushed
1 large red bell pepper, diced
2 medium potatoes, diced
1 large carrot, diced
1 sprig thyme
2 (15 ounce) cans white beans (such as cannellini)
2 cups chicken broth or vegetable broth
salt and pepper to taste

DIRECTIONS
1. Heat 1 tablespoon of the oil in a pot over medium heat. Add the chorizo and cook until browned throughout, about five minutes. Remove chorizo and place on a plate.
2. Heat the remaining tablespoon of oil in the pot. Reduce heat to low and add the onion, garlic, bell pepper, potatoes, carrot, and thyme. Cook and stir 3–5 minutes or until the onion becomes transparent.
3. Add the beans and broth to the pot. Simmer over medium heat until the vegetables are thoroughly cooked, about 8–10 minutes. Add water if you want a thinner stew. Mix the chorizo slices into the stew. Season with salt and pepper, and serve.

Makes 4 servings.

Mexican Iced Chocolate

Chocolate has a long history in Mexico, dating all the way back to the Aztecs! The Aztecs ground cacao seeds with vanilla and chili pepper to make a bitter drink they called *xocolatl* [shuck-OH-lahtl]. Today, children enjoy chocolate drinks similar to this one. Whip up a batch and see what you think. If you're brave, add the cayenne pepper for an extra spicy kick!

INGREDIENTS

4 cups milk
1 1/3 cup chocolate chips
2 teaspoons vanilla extract
1/2 teaspoon ground cinnamon
dash ground cayenne pepper (optional)
4 cinnamon sticks
ice cubes
whipped cream (optional)

DIRECTIONS

1. Combine the milk, chocolate chips, vanilla extract, ground cinnamon, and cayenne pepper in a saucepan over low heat. Stir constantly until the chocolate chips are melted.
2. Remove the mixture from heat and cool completely.
3. Fill four cups with ice cubes and pour the chocolate mixture into the cups.
4. Place a cinnamon stick in each cup.
5. Place a dollop of whipped cream on top of the chocolate mixture in each cup. Enjoy!

Makes 4 servings.

Pastel de Tres Leches

Tres means "three" in Spanish, and *leche* means "milk," so this dessert is a cake with three kinds of milk in it.

INGREDIENTS
1 ½ cups flour
1 teaspoon baking powder
⅛ teaspoon salt
⅓ cup vegetable oil
1 cup sugar
1 teaspoon vanilla extract
5 eggs
½ cup whole milk
½ cup heavy cream
1 can (12 ounces) evaporated milk
1 can (14 ounces) sweetened condensed milk
¾ cup whipped cream

DIRECTIONS
1. Preheat oven to 325 degrees.
2. Grease and flour a 9-inch by 13-inch baking pan.
3. Combine flour, baking powder, and salt.
4. In a separate bowl, combine oil, sugar, and vanilla extract.
5. Stir the eggs into the sugar mixture.
6. Stir in the milk, then gently fold in the flour mixture a little at a time.
7. Pour this batter into the pan and bake for 30–40 minutes or until it feels firm and a toothpick inserted into the center comes out clean.
8. Let the cake cool, then turn it out onto a serving platter and pierce it in several places with a fork. Let the cake cool in the refrigerator for an additional 30 minutes.
9. While the cake is cooling, whisk together the heavy cream, evaporated milk, and sweetened condensed milk.
10. Pour the cream mixture over the cake and cover with whipped cream.

Guatemalan Tostadas

Tostadas are a favorite food throughout Central America, although each country has its own twist on the dish. This recipe is for Guatemalan-style tostadas.

INGREDIENTS

6 flour tortillas, fried (see directions below)
beans (see directions below)
fresh guacamole (see directions below)
1 jar (16 ounces) salsa
1 cup white cheese, such as Monterey Jack, shredded

DIRECTIONS FOR FRYING THE TORTILLAS

Pour about ¼ cup vegetable oil in a skillet and heat it on medium-high. Place each tortilla in the oil and fry each side until it's crispy. Set the tortillas on paper towels to drain.

DIRECTIONS FOR THE BEANS

Combine the following ingredients in a pot over medium heat, stirring often, until most of the liquid evaporates:
1 tablespoon butter
¼ cup chopped onion (about ½ small onion)
¼ cup chopped red or green bell pepper (about ½ small pepper)
1 can (16 ounces) black beans
2 tablespoons water
salt to taste

DIRECTIONS FOR THE GUACAMOLE

Combine the following ingredients in a bowl:
2 medium avocados, peeled and mashed
¼ cup chopped onion
1 teaspoon salt
1 teaspoon black pepper
1 teaspoon fresh lemon juice (about ¼ lemon)

DIRECTIONS FOR PUTTING IT ALL TOGETHER

Spread about ¼ cup of the beans on a tortilla. Add a scoop of guacamole and a scoop of salsa, then sprinkle with some cheese. Enjoy!

Makes 6 tostadas.

Brigadeiro

Brigadeiro (pronounced bree-gah-dare-oh) is a special sweet treat for children in Brazil. Mix up a batch to give to your friends!

INGREDIENTS

1 can (14 ounces) sweetened condensed milk
½ cup unsweetened cocoa powder
1 teaspoon butter plus additional for greasing hands
sprinkles, shredded coconut, cocoa powder, chopped nuts, or powdered sugar
40 mini baking cups

DIRECTIONS

1. In a medium pan, cook the condensed milk, cocoa powder, and butter over medium heat.
2. Cook, stirring constantly, for about 10 minutes.
3. Remove the pan from the stove and let the mixture cool.
4. Grease your hands with some butter and roll the mixture into one-inch balls.
5. Roll each ball in sprinkles, shredded coconut, cocoa powder, chopped nuts, or powdered sugar.
6. Place each ball into its own mini baking cup. Enjoy, and refrigerate any leftovers!

Makes about 40 balls.

Colombian Arepas

Kids in South American countries such as Colombia love these corn-flour cakes. You can slice the cooked cakes in half and fill them with cheese, beans, or meat.

INGREDIENTS

1 teaspoon salt
2 cups masa flour (precooked corn flour, also called instant corn flour)
2¼ cups warm water
2 tablespoons butter, melted
3 tablespoons oil or nonstick cooking spray

DIRECTIONS

1. Stir the salt into the flour. Slowly add the water and mix to form dough. Add the butter and knead the dough until it's smooth but not sticky, adding water or flour as needed. Cover the dough with plastic wrap and let it sit for 15 minutes.
2. Divide the dough into about 20 pieces, rolling each into a ball. Flatten the balls into discs about the size of your palm and ¼ inch thick.
3. Coat a skillet with cooking spray and place it over medium heat. Place several arepas in the skillet and cook about five minutes per side. They should form a crust but shouldn't quite turn brown before you remove them. Eat them while they're warm, with or without filling.

Makes about 20 arepas.

Peruvian Potatoes with Huancaína

Huancaína (pronounced wan-ki-EE-nah) is a cheese sauce named for Huancayo, a city in the Peruvian highlands. This Peruvian dish was first made in 1870 when the railroad was built through towns in the Andes Mountains. Cooks used a small stone to blend the ingredients since they didn't have any electricity.

INGREDIENTS

4–5 medium potatoes, washed and sliced into thick rounds
½ pound Monterey Jack cheese, cut into chunks
½ hot pepper, washed, chopped, and with seeds removed
1 cup evaporated milk
¼ cup vegetable oil
1 garlic clove
salt and pepper to taste

DIRECTIONS

1. Place the potatoes in a medium-sized pot and cover with water. Bring the water to a boil and cook potatoes for about 10 minutes or until soft.
2. . Blend the cheese, pepper, evaporated milk, oil, garlic, salt, and pepper in a blender. If the sauce is too thick, add more milk.
3. Drain potatoes and place in a serving bowl. Pour cheese sauce over the potatoes and serve.

Makes 4 servings.

HELPING CHILDREN FALL IN LOVE WITH JESUS SO THEY CAN FALL IN LOVE WITH THE WORLD.

Children all over the world have the same needs: to be known, loved, cared for, and protected.

For some children, having these needs met is a delightful reality. But for many others, it is almost impossible to experience, because extreme poverty tells them they don't matter. Although poverty is often measured materially, it spills out emotionally and spiritually as well.

Jesus had compassion on the poor. When your children love Jesus and see the world through His eyes, compassion is a God-inspired response to need. Tyndale and Compassion International come together to create resources to help children fall in love with Jesus so they can follow His example to love others—especially those who live in poverty.

YOUR LOVE FOR ONE ANOTHER WILL PROVE TO THE WORLD THAT YOU ARE MY DISCIPLES. —JOHN 13:35

Releasing children from poverty
Compassion®
in Jesus' name

CP1473

LEAF A MESSAGE

Copy these leaves and cut them out to use with the "Leaf A Message" activity on page 62.

"PIECES OF THE WHOLE" TANGRAM TEMPLATE

Cut out the shapes to the left to use with the "Pieces of the Whole" activity on page 7.

...to use with the "Pieces of the Whole" activity on page 7.

FRIENDS AROUND THE WORLD

TANGRAM PUZZLE

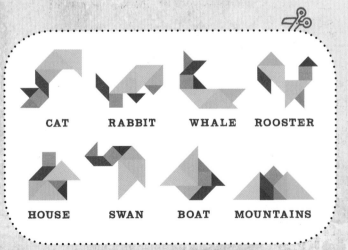

CAT	RABBIT	WHALE	ROOSTER

HOUSE	SWAN	BOAT	MOUNTAINS

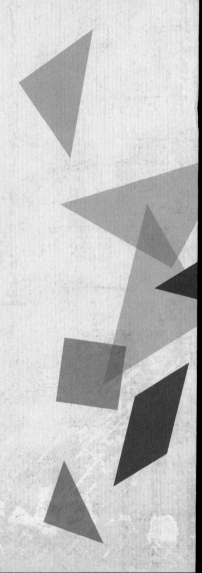